This Notebook Belongs to

Made in United States
North Haven, CT
15 June 2025

69831572R00057